The Master Coach Model

J. Arthur Smith, D.Min.

Where does the term "coaching" come from? We still use the term "coach" when referring to travel, be it airliner, train, stagecoach . . . as far back as the European coach. This was an early means of transportation, moving people from one place to another . . . and usually royal company. Thus, the etymology of the term "coaching" is moving people to where they choose to go—in style! Learn the art of coaching as you move and lead people—using *The Master Coach Model*.

About Leadership Systems, Inc. (LSI)

Dr. J. Arthur Smith and the LSI Team serve both individuals and organizations through leadership and executive coaching, assessment, training, and program development and design. Applying the experience of a professional leadership team whose work spans nearly all 50 states and 45 countries, we stand ready to assist you or your organization in attaining your professional and personal goals.

The professionals at LSI know that today's leaders face increasingly complex problems that require resourceful and innovative leadership training. Dr. Smith and associates invite you to discover what effective coaching can do for your career and business. The LSI approach to training and coaching includes:

- Highly customized programs
- Cutting-edge assessment tools
- Proven methodology and curriculum for leadership training
- Value-added follow-up and focus sessions

You can contact us at

LEADERSHIP SYSTEMS, INC.
607 Greenwood Drive
High Point, North Carolina 27262

PHONE: 336.869.0850
FAX: 336.869.5693
EMAIL: Lead@LeadershipSystems.com

Table of Contents

Front cover photo used by permission.
Royal Collection Trust / ©Her Majesty Queen Elizabeth II 2015; Photographer: David Cripps
Back cover photo used by permission - Patrick Jinks
Cover design by Chris Hollingsworth - Fresh Graphic Juice

ISBN No. 978-0-9962988-0-3

THE MASTER COACH

I have been coaching executives now for 27 years. One of my observations is that the most productive years in terms of contribution, content, and wisdom seems to be one's fifties. I am now at that point in life. I reached the milestone of 10,000 coaching sessions in July of 2011 and am continuing to add to that number. And so it became apparent to me that it may be time to write about my experience in this field.

Since 1989, I have been an adjunct trainer and coach with the Center for Creative Leadership (CCL®), a world-class, top-ranked, global provider of executive education that unlocks individual and organizational potential through its exclusive focus on leadership development and research (*Bloomberg BusinessWeek*). I was honored to be selected as the coach for CCL's coach-training video. After being selected for their most senior coaching programs, Leadership at the Peak and The Looking Glass Experience, I was invited to travel to Switzerland to continue my coaching. Then I realized that I could be of use to others in their coaching pursuits.

A quarter of a century of good ratings at the Center for Creative Leadership has paid off. I find myself turning down more opportunities to work, both nationally and internationally, as my schedule continues to overflow. My ambition is for this book to serve as a manual to train others in the tools, techniques, methods, and metaphors that have become very useful to me in my coaching sessions.

My coaching expertise has been gained through my experiences with CCL and Leadership Systems, Inc. (LSI), the company I began in 1992 in

High Point, North Carolina. Coaching has become my love and my professional passion. The process of helping others understand CCL's motto—"Leadership, Learning, Life"—has also been my focus over the past two decades. My aim at LSI is to coach in a manner that my clients not only remember, but in a way that they can never forget!

THE MASTER COACH CONCEPT

I have coached leaders from nearly all 50 states and 45 countries. I have developed a workable perspective with context, experience, and results. The unique distinction that I bring results from my doctoral dissertation on the key question categories that I use in coaching.

This approach is explained in the following pages and is useful in the professional coaching world, educational fields, other management levels, and even in the home.

The approach is known in our organization as *The Master Coach Model*. Most commonly associated with the Greek philosopher Socrates, the ancient Socratic method was familiar to people of the ancient world. The method of teaching with questions actually predates Socrates, but was popularized by him and had its fullest expression in the Roman Era.

In contrast to that of Western civilization, the Eastern way of thinking is far more reflective and internal. Today's Western culture is more linear and "left brain," using rational question-and-answer approaches. The teacher or coach usually has the answer and the student is tasked with answering what the teacher knows, or by guessing what the teacher is thinking. This more traditional way of learning has some value. What is sacrificed is the student's role in thinking, processing, and the notion of buy-in—i.e., giving support to an answer or conclusion as a result of having involvement in its formulation.

The Eastern way of thinking allows for much more processing time because more contemplation is involved. Thus, the Master Coaching approach allows for and even provokes the same. This method is designed around questions: questions from stem to stern, top to bottom, and beginning to end.

Questions are the essence of *The Master Coach Model*. Why questions? Well, an interesting question, don't you think? Why do you think this method is based on questions? The method of asking questions is practiced here to provoke curiosity, to open your mind, and to create hunger to explore the answers.

In the spirit of this learning approach, take a break here, do not read further, and think this question through. Instead of racing ahead to the answer, stop, reflect, listen, and discover.

—It takes more brain power to process questions and think. This is like working out the brain instead of spoon-feeding it. The information is meditated on and processed and internalized.

> # Questions are the essence of *The Master Coach Model*. Why questions? Well, an interesting question, don't you think?

WHAT IS THE VALUE OF ASKING A MORE REFLECTIVE QUESTION?

Questions are the critical foundation
of *The Master Coach Model*.

? Questions focus on the answer coming from the coachee (student or employee) and not the coach (teacher or supervisor).

? Questions frame the issue and align the key factors, but do not conclude. They insinuate, suggest, and maybe hint, but questions also can be simple, powerful, and strong. Questions are especially well suited when the answer is not known or the solution is not clear.

? The right *kind* of question, not the actual question, brings the optimal answer. Questions must be in an interactive and developing dialogue.

? The essence of the question can bring the best out of the coachee. The best answers to complicated issues usually emerge after careful thought, rather than hurried response.

? The best questions result in some of the best solutions. The added benefit of "buy-in," and commitment to the solution, tends to come when the solutions emerge from the coachee.

? Good questions frame solutions through the one asked, facilitating a person's best learning, rather than simply asking the person to guess what the teacher is thinking.

? Questions can be memorable, and sometimes unforgettable.

? Questions pull innovation, creative thinking, and discovery, which is critical in a rapidly changing world.

? This method of learning is repeatable. A student of this method can transfer the learning process onto others.

? Questioning is fertile soil for the development of a relationship. Other means of learning can be coercion, data dump, and lecture. This method is the preferred relational building model for enjoyable and long-term relationships.

? Finally, questions are better because they allow for optimal learning where both the teacher (coach) and the student (coachee) can learn together and provide the collaboration necessary to effectively solve complex situations.

Questions pull innovation, creative thinking, and discovery, which is critical in a rapidly changing world.

What Is Coaching?

Coaching is a form of leadership that demands the right mind-set. This mind-set is a framing, facilitative way of thinking and one that usually drives the coach to provide questions, not answers. One of the greatest challenges in coaching is getting into the mind-set of coaching. This mind-set seems particularly hard in our American culture, as we are so committed to efficiency and practical, fast solutions. In the early days of most careers the "right answer" is often what the boss, or leader, says or wants, period. As a career progresses, the challenges are greater, and the need for the employee rather than the supervisor to solve problems increases because the employee is closer to the issue.

Coaching Closest to the Issue

Who do you think is most likely to be the best problem solver? Is it not the one closest to the issue who is tasked with solving the problem, and therefore motivated to find a solution? The boss, leader, counselor, or coach dispensing the answer while in a position of greater wisdom is rarely the best approach. Certainly that approach is the least motivational and least educational.

Even early in one's career, the employee is probably still the best one to solve a problem. The best role for the manager or coach is to frame, reflect, and guide with questions. The tendency for most employees is simply to do what they are told. The habit of doing, rather than thinking and solving the problem, becomes the habit of both the employee and the manager.

THE COACHING MIND-SET

How can I assist the coachee to see, to solve, and to think for himself? If you are in this mind-set, you are ready to coach. If you are not, then these effective coaching techniques will fall short. A good surgeon performing an operation while tired, angry, or distracted may still be a good surgeon. However, the operation performed when his or her mind is not in the right place is likely to be less than perfect. Coaching can be analogous. If you approach a coaching opportunity without the right mind-set, your efforts are likely to bring more harm than improvement.

The right mind-set is critical. The right mind-set brings about attempts to pull the solution from the coachee, rather than to drive the coach's predetermined solution. In a situation where the coaching mind-set is not in play, the coach should call a time-out, delay the meeting, or take a break until he is ready to genuinely coach with *The Master Coach Model*.

The focus of coaching with *The Master Coach Model* is to develop the coachees through teaching and training, not only to get the answer or solution this time, but also to adopt *The Master Coach Model* themselves so that they may pass on the method.

With each new day the world is moving faster and the business environment is becoming more global. *The Master Coach Model*'s unique problem-solving focus provides the most efficient means to adapt to quickly evolving operations. The process of coaching with the right mind-set is an interactive method to guide the coachee to an answer. This model is particularly useful and powerful when the coach may not know the answer or solution.

MODELING THE MASTER MODEL

When the coach knows the answer, the empowerment and confidence of the coachee soars if he or she can verbalize the answer. But when the coach doesn't have the answer and must pull it from the coachee via focused questioning, this method is the best route to a viable and owned solution. A coaching assignment in San Francisco with medical professionals illustrates this style of coaching. I have wondered many times on the flight from North Carolina to California: "Why am I traveling coast to coast to conduct a 75-minute session with this physician?" I was thinking of how many leadership coaches may be flying over, and how many coaches who could do what I was going to do the next day may be right there in San Francisco.

Although most of my coaching has been developmental in nature, occasionally a client is so preoccupied with a current challenge that he leaps into the issue confronting him. In the client's mind, it is this big issue that must be solved and that is inhibiting his success. As I listened to this brilliant and highly educated senior manager of many medical professionals, he explained in a very articulate way the complicated situation he faced. He was eloquent in his explanation.

I demonstrated *The Master Coach Model* with these words: "Wow, Doc, you really have a significant challenge here, and you so clearly have articulated it to me." (Actually, he took over 40 minutes of our 75 minutes just to introduce himself and to explain his problem using vocabulary, nomenclature, and acronyms that I had little or no understanding of.) I continued by saying, "First of all, I can tell that you are very sharp, and secondly that you have thought about your dilemma a lot."

Indeed, he was one of the most intelligent people that I have ever met. To this point in the coaching session I had not contributed to solving the problem. I had validated the dilemma, and at least made the client feel it was significant. When coachees feel heard and validated, this relieves them of the need to further explain, and from the need to convince the coach that they have a big challenge on their hands.

Next, I asked him a question to refocus the discussion on taking action to solve the problem instead of giving him any idea that I would be the problem solver. Not only would an action plan developed by the coachee be carried out more effectively, but in this case a coachee-created solution was the only option. In this scenario the coachee was the only person with the requisite specialized knowledge to develop any solution at all.

I then proceeded by asking, "Doc, am I right that you have spent many hours thinking about this challenge and contemplating many solutions?" He assured me that he had. Then I asked him the crucial question: "Doc, what could you do that until now you have never considered?" I was practicing the Master Model of coaching and hoping that he might, in the moment, come up with a new thought or idea for a workable solution. This was the case. He responded, "What could I do that I have never considered? I do not know, well wait, not until now, have I...never thought of this idea.... Man, you are brilliant. You are really worth your salary. I think I have it." No one was more relieved than I was at that moment. But the greater pleasure came as I witnessed the doctor, who initially was fully convinced that he had an unsolvable situation, be transformed into a very different, very motivated, and very excited client looking toward what to him was a plausible and workable solution. And do you know the best part? I still do not know what he was talking about.

Is it ideal to coach in an arena in which the coach has very limited knowledge? No, but it happens. This situation becomes more frequent in a quickly changing world. A good coach can practice *The Master Coach Model* of coaching and skillfully use questions to assist another person's strategy, insight, solution, or perspective and yet the coach may not at all fully understand the problem.

Who do you think is most likely to be the best problem solver? Is it not the one closest to the issue? The one tasked with solving the problem and motivated to get the problem solved? For the boss, leader, counselor, or coach to dispense the answer in a position of greater wisdom is rarely the best approach. Certainly that approach is the least motivational and least educational. Oftentimes when using *The Master Coach Model*, the less information the coach has about an issue the better.

The "what" of coaching is a masterful process of discovery. It is the pulling and surfacing of awareness, thinking, and commitment of not just one idea, but many. (How many heads are better than one?)

This is particularly important as we see the world rapidly growing, changing, and gaining complexity at an alarming rate. Knowledge is multiplying at an ever increasing pace, and the once top-down, follow-the-expert approach and other traditionally successful ways of problem solving are sinking into obsolescence. *The Master Coach Model* has ancient roots, but remains contemporary.

WHEN CAN I USE COACHING?

After more than 12,500 one-on-one coaching sessions with profes-
sionals, hundreds of parenting conversations with my four children,
and interactions with my spouse (who is much smarter than I am),
I stay convinced that the *when* of coaching is most of the time. If
you want your listeners, students, or employees to really think, to dig
down deep, reflect, consider, and process, then *The Master Coach Model* is
incomparable. I have used this method in counseling very difficult situations, even those involving life and death. I have used this method in a
very quick sports moment, and in most, if not all, of my one-on-one sessions with senior executives.

Here are some examples where this method of coaching has been used.

FACING A CHALLENGE

I have used the questioning method with even very young children, and
will never forget my son, still in middle school, using *The Master Coach*
Model on me. I was about to leave the house and had one of those more
transparent moments as I told him that I was feeling uneasy about the big
seminar of the day. After commenting that I was a bit nervous, he asked,
"Is there anyone else who knows as much as you on the topic you are
speaking about?" I said that there probably is someone somewhere, but
that I knew the information very well. Then he asked, "Do you think anyone there will know more than you about it?" I responded, "Well, probably
not." He questioned further by asking, "Then why are you nervous?" He

had me there. Through his simple, well-worded questions he had coached me. As I answered these questions I owned the new thinking and the reality that seemed to surface through verbally expressing the words. I could not deny my own answer, and it had the effect of changing my perspective and my emotions.

A SEEMINGLY IMPOSSIBLE SITUATION

This method of coaching was used on me another memorable time by a new hire. He was offering the services of Leadership Systems, Inc., to a client. Being his first day at work, he was doing well but could only sell utilizing the client assessment mode because he knew little about our products and services. Asking questions about the needs of the clients was about all he could do. He did well with that interrogative approach, as he landed the head of training for GTE (later Verizon) Communications. He asked lots of questions and discovered that they were only a few weeks away from their National Sales Trainer Seminar in beautiful Sedona, Arizona. He asked if all of the sessions were fully staffed, or if another speaker or vendor might be considered. The head of training clearly told him that there was no need at this time, then went on to talk about the great training setup and the high quality of the seminar planned in Sedona. My teammate wisely told her that we really would add another dimension to the training, yet he could say little as he was not yet adequately informed as to the LSI capabilities, or of precisely what she needed. But he did manage to say that we were so interested that we would be there in the morning to complete the discussion.

As I listened, I was initially impressed at both his questions and his confidence and assertiveness. But my good impression turned to disbelief as he told me he had committed us both to be there in the morning, which would necessitate us departing our homes no later than 2:00 a.m. to comfortably be at the corporate offices in Atlanta by 7:30 the next morning, our scheduled appointment time. I told him there was no way I could be there and that he would have to go alone. He wisely practiced *The Master Coach Model* of coaching on me by first validating my position and then systematically asking me questions until I saw it differently, made a change of mind, and enthusiastically decided to be with the team and go to Atlanta.

He proceeded, "You probably have good reasons for not going with me to call on one of the top communications phone companies in the world. What are they?" He patiently listened as I told him that I had several appointments the next day, I had not planned to go, and besides, I had not told my wife that I would be traveling. The change of schedule would change my whole family's schedule. He responded, "Jim, do you think that at this stage I can adequately represent your company?" I said, "No." He admitted the loss of business that might be associated with my cancellations on the next day, but paralleled the potential loss of business to the potential gain with the question, "If we are successful and get the assignment to go and get the opportunity to teach and coach the nation's top sales trainers from across the USA, what might that mean in total revenue to LSI?" I could only concede that it would probably be very valuable, and the connections and exposure alone would be worthwhile. Finally, he moved me to the place of commitment, as he asked if there was anyone besides me that could present the offerings of LSI better than Jim Smith, the founder and president. After the anticipated answer, he cleaned up the victory by asking if his arrival with coffee and food when I awoke, with him taking the role of driver, would be okay.

I agreed. We made the drive, got the business, and had a memorable time of training and interaction at The Enchantment Resort in Sedona. This training experience, that I almost missed, is now one of my fondest professional memories.

Staying in the facilitator's role and using *The Master Coach Model* was the key, so as to pull from the coachee and not add to the coachee's insights and ideas, until it was time to make some connections.

PERFECT OVER THE HUDSON

People often push back at *The Master Coach Model* by saying things like it's "too slow," "too Southern," or "not practical if you're in a rush or the stakes are high"! The powerful story of January 15, 2009, speaks to using this model even in such situations.

US Airways Captain Chesley "Sully" Sullenberger and his crew on Flight 1549 had a big problem. The jet engines hit a flock of geese and immediately failed. So why was he "perfect over the Hudson"? Obviously he did what no other pilot had successfully done. He made a safe water landing. But what else did he do that was deemed "perfect"?

Imagine that situation—41 seconds into the flight, and now your plane is disabled, only gliding, and not for long. He called and reported to the

LaGuardia Tower, not once or twice but three times, that he would be landing in the Hudson. Not only did he think clearly, glide expertly, and communicate calmly to the slow-to-understand FAA controller in the tower, but he did something else. What was it?

Capt. Sullenberger did something that most pilots in a very serious situation would not think of doing. In his very busy seconds with the lives of 150 plus passengers, his flight crew, and himself in peril, he did something that has been referred to as almost "perfect." In these situations, most crew members will support well, and comply with the orders of the captain. The crew will be cooperative and willing, but often refrain from interrupting due to high stress with which the captain or boss is dealing. In this case, he was gliding a very heavy and disabled plane, communicating with a seemingly hard-to-hear FAA controller, and handling other necessary emergency procedures. In such situations the staff will rarely offer a suggestion, unless asked directly. This is what Capt. Sullenberger did, and this is what was deemed "perfect."

Capt. Sullenberger actually leveraged his crew and asked his copilot, in those moments of impending disaster and potential death, "Got any ideas?" to which the copilot, Jeffrey Skiles, replied, "Actually not." You see, he was perfect, because the copilot may have seen a vacant but optional airstrip or landing field that the captain did not see. The copilot may have assumed that the pilot had ruled it out, and thus was silent. Had there been an optional landing field, it may have been the better choice, but in this case, there wasn't one. But what made the pilot perfect? His ability to manage the stress, fly the plane, communicate with all necessary personnel, including his copilot (the next best one to have a solution) by asking him a quick, but valuable question. He actually coached his copilot in that moment. He used the question to pull any potential solutions, and at the least, obtained the copilot's full cooperation in the direction in which they were quickly and dangerously heading. He used the team approach, and *The Master Coach Model*, quickly but effectively to consult all reasonable answers and thus was "Perfect over the Hudson."

When NOT to Use *The Master Coach Model*

There are some circumstances in which *The Master Coach Model* is *not* the right approach:

× When there is a question of integrity, safety, or morality on the line and you are asked "point blank" for your answer,

× During a crisis, such as a building on fire, and it is clearly not a time for questions,

× When the issue is one that is dictated by the organization and the goals have been previously set for the coachee, and

× When you as the coach are not in the coaching mind-set and are trying to drive and push rather than pull from the coachee.

In the examples above, the situations where using *The Master Coach Model* is inappropriate are when the answer is already clearly known, stated, or required by the organization, or by the situation or values. These situations need no exploring or *pulling* from the coach.

So the "when" of coaching may be on a continuum from often to almost always. The only times when it is not wise to use the method is when there is no time, no benefit, or an incorrect mind-set. A burning building is another true emergency. Any available leadership is desirable, and the faster and more accurate the instruction, the better. The firefighter who finds me in a smoke-filled building would not be encouraging, motivational, or smart to say, "So where do you think an exit might be located?" When people are in shock, fear, or panic, they simply need to be told, "This is your way to safety" or "go to that exit" or "come here." This is the time for the Nike philosophy, "Just Do It."

In the movie *Saving Private Ryan*, there was the tense moment of truth when the squad of men was demoralized after losing its medic in a tough battle. The lieutenant had the rank and authority to simply order them forward, but even that power of position had its limitations, and he knew he needed them to be committed if they were to move ahead with him. So he used some interaction, some questions, and was masterfully able to bring them all back to a place of unity, commitment, and trust, even in the face of death.

Those who followed Christ, likewise, saw some very discouraging days, and in their moment of truth the master leader, Jesus, invited them to consider departing and turning back from their mission. The followers showed their commitment by answering His question with a question: "And to whom shall we go? Only You have words of eternal life." In the face of this now personal revelation, not told to do something or persuaded by the leader's rhetoric, they showed their commitment to continue on and to wholeheartedly follow their leader.

Why Should I Use *The Master Coach Model?*

Master Coaching is not only effective, motivating, and wise, but it also maintains the greatest amount of one's integrity and respect. Attempting to solve another's challenges is often prideful at best, and in error at worst. When you attempt to solve another's problem without clarifying and affirming questions, and assurance that you understand the complexity of the situation, you risk the coachee's confidence. This demotivation of another is one of the principal reasons for high attrition in organizations, and a lack of teamwork and synergy.

The rapidly changing culture is another reason for using *The Master Coach Model* in coaching. Given today's complexities, the question approach to coaching offers more teamwork and insight for the best solution. But there is also another reason. The "millennial minds" of today tend to assign almost immediate irrelevance to the mind that offers any dated data, ideas, or solutions. A rapidly changing world is more likely to use more relevant solutions, but a dated idea is not necessarily irrelevant. On the contrary, it may be the best, tried and true, and most accurate solution. However, motivated younger mind tends to discount it. *The Master Coach Model* has the potential to draw out the best answer from the coachee and to extract its relevance. It allows the coach to align that newer, or at least perceived newer, solution with their known or tried solution, and proceed with "win-win" collaboration.

How many times have you made a great suggestion, offered a solution, or given an answer, only to see it fall on deaf ears? How many times has this approach simply not worked, and our assertions or statements failed to have any impact? Was it because it had been tried? Was it too simple to cope with the complexity? Or did the power of the fast response somehow affect the opposite of your intentions? Many factors can be at play to discount the coach's answer or ideas.

Questions invite, explore, and sometimes require the coachee to think. The coachee is requested to turn the tumblers of her mind and to unlock her ideas, perspective, and insight in order to move them to a different place and to frame the issue under discussion in a much different light. If the coach is asserting, suggesting, pushing, or teaching, the perspective switch often fails to turn on. When the doors do not unlock in the coachee's mind, then the coach is simply back to telling, selling, and convincing the coachee of the coach's own perspective.

The Master Coach Model fully utilizes the gifts, knowledge, skills, vision, and character of the one coached. This method, though a bit slower than the traditional Western top-down approach, has more staying power. It allows for more combined wisdom, more potential for unity, synergy, and syzygy than any other coaching method or psychological theory. The question-asking approach was used by Jesus and Socrates and remains the time-honored classic among law professors.

Whether it is Socrates' ambition to enlighten others primarily by using questions, or Jesus posing the question to his followers, "Who do others say that I am?" both are helping others realize how they have come to their conclusions. President Kennedy directing us to "ask not what your country can do for you—ask what you can do for your country" uses the question as a tool for encouraging the listener to think or to act differently.

The result of this model based on questions is reflection, deep consideration, and thinking that usually results in action being taken, or at least a different perspective being formed.

These types of questions do not leave; they stay with us, sleep with us, and sometimes wake us. They prick and probe and even disturb us. At a minimum, they put us at a likely place of change, action, and nonequilibrium. This is the place past complacency, the lobby of change, and often the place of a new decision that will not simply stay in the mind. It finds application and execution.

In coaching senior global executives, leaders, and managers around the world, the *why* of coaching is obvious. These people are smart, sharp, and not only *could* solve their own problems, but *should* solve them. They often tell me they need to show others how to do the same. But this ideal is often mired in the complexity, distractions, and pressure of the moment. A coach is there to allow focus, offer clarity, raise their awareness, and keep them on track.

The *why* of coaching is not just because the coachees should be the ones to find the solutions, but they are often the only ones that can. To think that a coach, or even a senior boss, could just drop by and hear a sizeable problem and simply solve it with a brief answer is not only hard to believe, but is actually a pretty arrogant approach. The chances are that they would provoke more than an eye roll, a discouraged but respectful sigh, or a quiet, "Yes, sir." But deep down the emotion that is wrapped up in the honest response, if it could be uttered, would be, "You just don't get it, do you boss? If it was that simple, I would never have brought you into the problem." This response is common. This may be avoided with a few more seconds of patience, a few suitable questions, and some invitations to think deeper to see why the initial approach did not completely succeed.

Finally, a manager who takes the time to invite employees onward to a "win-win" solution will be encouraging those employees to develop answers that they will remember, that they will take ownership in, and they will then create momentum toward enacting the solution.

> The best problem-solving results come from exploring the coachee's solutions rather than immediately offering the coach's solution. Problems are best solved by the person closest to the problem.

How Do I Coach?

The *how* of coaching is best explained in the Leadership Coaching Training Seminar (LCT). This seminar, led by Leadership Systems, Inc. (LSI), is an action oriented and facilitated workshop that trains leaders in *The Master Coach Model*. This is the first step in becoming a Leadership Coach with LSI.

The model (see next page) is broken down into three phases: Phase 1 – Discussion Phase, Phase 2 – Discovery Phase, and Phase 3 – Decision Phase. These phases are described in the following pages.

THE MASTER COACH MODEL

LEADERSHIP
SYSTEMS

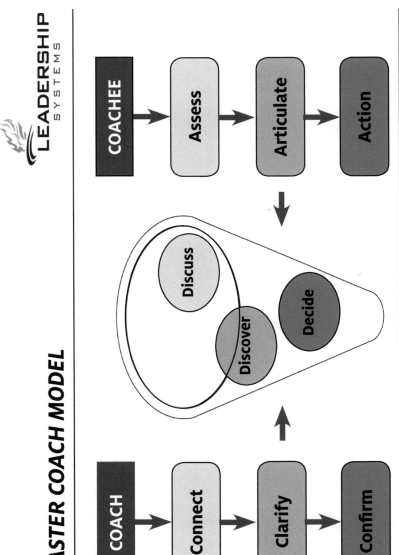

(Metaphor)

© 2015 Leadership Systems, Inc.

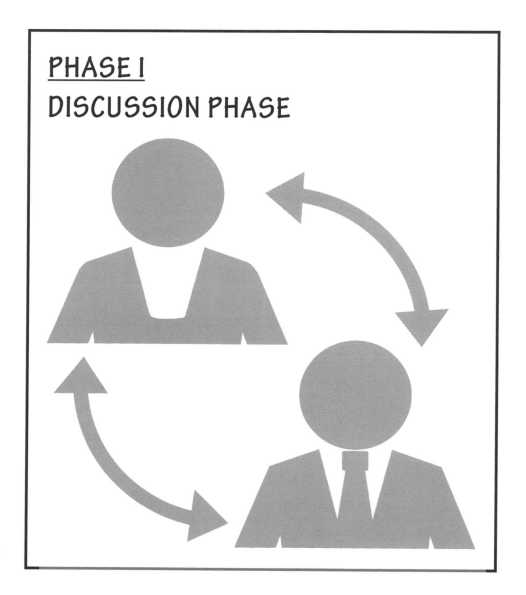

PHASE I
DISCUSSION PHASE

THE COACH – CONNECT

The coach must make a sincere effort to Connect. In order to foster open and honest communication the coachee must sense the coach's sincerity and desire to truly listen to what he or she is saying. The coach must approach the situation while being in the right mind-set, which is to facilitate, to develop, to frame, to pull, and to discover. The coachee must also come in a mind-set of willingness. Often in the initial moments of a coaching session, as you begin your initial assessment and in the first few questions, there might be good reason to halt, postpone, or refocus the session.

THE COACHEE – ASSESS

The coachee must not only come in the right mind-set of openness and willingness to work on an issue, he or she must primarily focus on Assessment. Too often the coach has conducted the assessment alone. When the coach assesses the issue alone, he will be hours if not days ahead of the mental and emotional state of the coachee. This simple reality explains most of the frustration that comes as a result of a coach or boss asking the coachee or employee for an answer or solution and the coachee simply offering the "deer in the headlights" frozen response or a low quality and somewhat noncreative solution. The assessment step often takes some time on the part of the coachee and patience on the part of the coach. The coachee has to assess what the problem or challenge really is and take a deeper look at the issue from more than one perspective. As the assessment takes place, the coach often wants to jump to ideas or solutions. However, this is premature, because the coachee has only been thinking about this issue for seconds or minutes.

Once the assessment of the issue or problem has been made, the coachee must then keep articulation of the issue in mind as the coach and coachee discuss it together.

TOGETHER – DISCUSS

The coach and coachee continue into the Discussion step to clearly identify the issue, challenge, or problem. The coach attempts to pull with questions to keep the coachee focused. When the coach brings the issue, challenge, or problem to the table through questions, the motivation to work on it is much higher for the coachee than when the coach simply announces the issue to be discussed.

The coach not only clarifies the issue to be discussed but also continues working to pull out potential ideas and solutions that might be the way to work toward resolution of the issue or problem. This continuance of pulling with questions and the technique of keeping the coachee focused on articulation of the issue and the potential solution is the fundamental basis of this coaching style.

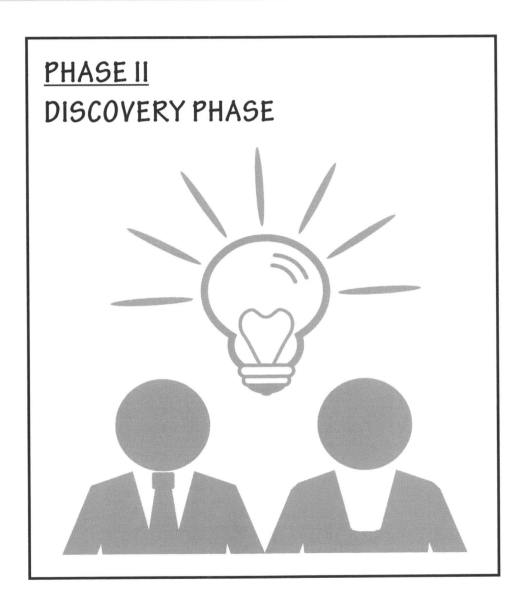

PHASE II
DISCOVERY PHASE

THE COACH – CLARIFY

This is a Clarifying step, in which the observations, challenges, or problems are clarified, explored, and investigated. The coach must assist and team up with the coachee to gain clarity. The power of questions and maintaining the coachee's curiosity cannot be underestimated in this phase, for questions are the coach's best tools.

Not only must the coach ask questions, but he must also perform a higher quality of listening. We, at Leadership Systems, Inc., call it "listening to understand." When a coach listens to understand he is able to accurately *rephrase* what was said, as opposed to merely listening to give a response. Pause and reflect: The last time you were in a discussion were you listening to understand, or listening for a place to "get in"?

Too often in a coaching discussion the coach is only listening for a moment and interrupts the coachee's thoughts and discussion with an offering of his or her right answer, wisdom, or story. This, though well intended, is poor coaching, and it is certainly not *The Master Coach Model*.

THE COACHEE – ARTICULATE

This step, Articulate, comes as a result of the coach's good questions. The discussion proceeds around the issue or problem, but all too often the coach, in the greater leadership role, leads by doing most of the talking. This not only prohibits the coachee from articulating, but also prohibits him from thinking and reasoning at a deeper level. Even Albert Einstein said, "Problems cannot be solved at the same level of thinking that created them." Therefore, keeping the coachee talking or at least thinking is critical in this step. The coach is to clarify what is said, by rephrasing and restating, but not to offer suggestions or solutions. At this point, if a coachee is stuck and has no ideas for further questions, one powerful technique is simply to take a break, to reschedule, and to get back together the next day when he has had some time to think deeply, to consider, and to formulate an idea or solution worth articulating.

Once valuable articulation has been heard and rephrased by a skillful coach who has really been "listening to understand," the final step for the coachee is to commit to an action plan.

TOGETHER – DISCOVER

The coach and coachee must first assess the situation. Are they both in the right mind-set for coaching? Is the coach really ready to lead, to pull, and to discover with a curiosity that will allow the coachee to surface the solution? It is important to note that in the Discover step, the coach may discover that the coachee does not seem to be in the right mind-set to be coached. This may cause the coach to delay, to reschedule, and to wait for the right time for greater participation and subsequent success. In addition, the coach may not be in the right mind-set for coaching; if this is discovered, it is best to postpone the coaching session.

Together, the coach and coachee *discover* the issue, challenge, or problem. The coachee may bring the issue to the table and the coach discovers it through his questions, or the coach may bring the issue to the table and the coachee discovers the issue by the coach's setup or explanation of what she has seen as an important issue that needs to be discussed.

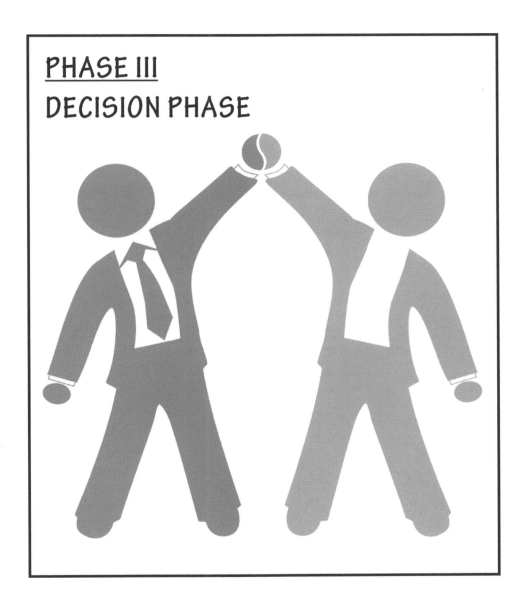

PHASE III
DECISION PHASE

THE COACH – CONFIRM

The third step of coaching is the Confirm step, which takes place during the critical Decision Phase. Without this step, one has simply had a good talk. The talk may have been personable, exploratory, and encouraging, but not actionable. Execution is more likely if the coach brings the coachee to the final step for confirmation and execution.

Finally, what is the coachee to focus on? The solution is above; it is woven throughout the process as already seen, but to make it even clearer, the coachee is to Assess, Articulate, and have a plan for Action.

THE COACHEE – ACTION

This step of Action seems obvious, but it is where most coaching derails. Even a patient coach, who has been effective so far, frequently jumps in to summarize and tell the coachee what she needs to do next. Although the coach, if he is the boss, may have the authority to do this, it is not a wise decision if he wants the action plan to be fully owned and executed by the coachee.

A repeated scenario when I am helping others to develop their skills in a coaching-training practice session proceeds like this:

> I am interrupted at the point of developing an action plan as the coach-in-training has taken the wheel and begins to tell, instruct, and summarize the action plan. I usually respond

to the interruption by saying, "Excuse me, whose action plan is this?" Obviously, I am making the point that because the coach is talking and taking the plan away it is now the coach's plan. The coach often sheepishly replies, "Well, it is mine..." as they realize that they are now doing the talking and have therefore hijacked the action plan from the brain and mouth of the coachee. I often add, "The coachee seems like a pretty smart person, and since he is closer to both the problem and the solution, can we let the coachee try to do the summary and action plan?"

The value of the coachee to verbally construct the action plan cannot be overemphasized. The coachee must not only articulate, but also literally construct the steps, priorities, and deliverables along with the time frame. This is a great time for the coach to step back to the Clarify step and to rephrase when appropriate. The coach may question if the plan is in any way off track or failing to align with other timetables, or if it is just not clear enough for success.

TOGETHER – DECIDE

The third step for the coach and coachee is to Decide. When a solution is on the table—a reasonable solution, owned by the coachee and validated by the coach—it is time for a decision to be made. The decision is about action, time frame, and commitment from the coachee. Often the coachee attempts to hook or delegate back to the coach at this point to request help.

The coach may ask:

Who is closer to the issue, you or me?

If you are successful in the full implementation of the solution, how might that enhance your career and future reputation as an effective employee?

These coaching attempts are to keep the focus on the coachee. Even though both the coach and coachee have a role in this process, the one responsible for creating the solution and for executing the solution is the coachee.

DISTINCTIONS OF *THE MASTER COACH MODEL*

What are the distinctions of *The Master Coach Model*? What makes this coaching different from other more direct models or methods of coaching? The answer is in the perspective. The best answers are *pulled* not *pushed*. The process is the interactive way of discovering the truth, the solution, or the plan of action. The perception is that the best answers are not from the coach, even if the coach could offer a faster, more efficient, and workable solution. The best answers must come from the coachee, because the answer is personal, designed and owned by the coachee.

An example of this is when one is being coached and the coachee seems stuck and not able to see the issue or find an answer. Especially when the coach thinks he has the answer, *The Master Coach Model* holds or reserves the answer. *The Master Coach Model* reminds the coach that the coach's answer may be one right answer, but it is the coach's answer and not yet owned and valued by the coachee. Therefore, the best approach for the coach may be to reserve that solution until the coachee does some thinking, research, or consideration of other possible or creative solutions. The coach affects this by asking, "Have you had some time to research or to consider other alternatives?" The coach may validate a given partial answer and then do a bit of "leading the horse to water," stopping short of stating the answer.

Another distinction in this model is that it is unforgettable. Most approaches to coaching are based more on the expert wisdom or knowledge from the coach or boss. This method requires the coachee to recall or remember what the coach said. *The Master Coach Model* is based on surfacing the answer from the coachee, thus making the method and the solution unforgettable.

A third distinction is that this model is very conducive to metaphors. Unforgettable coaching uses metaphor, and the best metaphor is drawn from the coachee. How many times have you reveled in the fact that it was your idea, your solution, or your thinking that was the key? How many times has your confidence grown as you realized that you did know the answer, but just needed it surfaced, validated, and heard by someone you trusted and reported to?

This style fosters confidence, satisfaction, and is easily remembered because it came from the one who must put it into action.

I have often said that metaphors are the crown of coaching. One of the best ways to make coaching more memorable, actually unforgettable, is to employ metaphor.

> Unforgettable coaching uses metaphor,
> and the best metaphor is drawn from the coachee.

USING METAPHORS IN COACHING

Metaphors are stories that are a good and valid comparison to what the coachee is describing or experiencing in life. The best metaphors are derived or surfaced from your client or coachee. The most fertile ground for locating an appropriate metaphor is one that the coachee knows well, has formerly experienced, or is currently living. That fertile ground is most often accessed through listening to the coachee and through the initial questions about the coachee's past, interests, hobbies, and passion. Often, the coachee will speak of sports, coaching sports, gardening, flying, travel, clubs or other community activities. The best metaphors come from this type of knowledge of former or current experiences.

My preference is to derive the metaphor from the coachee's actual words, when possible. Allow the coachee to tell you about basic interests and then suggest that the leadership learning might be much like their interest, hobby, or sport. It is imperative that you ask the coachee how the learning might be connected or otherwise illustrative of the interest, hobby, or sport.

Interactive metaphors are used to rephrase struggles and use questions while continuing the discussion and deepening the relationship with the coachee at the same time.

Here are some of my favorite metaphors.

Quarterback

My favorite and most frequently used metaphor, especially during football season and if the coachee has demonstrated an interest in football, is the Quarterback. A situation that might benefit from this metaphor is a classic scenario of a busy manager or executive who has been recently promoted to the next level and is finding his job very demanding. The obvious over-play of a good strength, working hard and getting much done alone, is no longer an effective strategy. This leader now needs to rethink his strategy. There is a requirement for delegation and a need to leverage others and to work smarter, not harder.

> **Coach:** As you think about your current role with all your tasks and demands, what offensive player in the backfield does it make you think of the most?

> **Coachee:** *Well, with all my busy work and assignments, I feel like I need to be a running back or maybe a fullback.*

> **Coach:** I bet you do, just trying to run hard and fast and get as much yardage as you can on each play, each day. What other player on the offense comes to mind, that seems more strategic?

Coachee: *The quarterback, I suppose.*

Coach: Yes, but tell me how. What does the QB think before the play begins?

Coachee: *Well, he calls some of the plays, reads the situation, the defensive lineup, and makes changes when he sees their specific formation, and sometimes calls a different play.*

Coach: Yes, and in terms of running the ball?

Coachee: *No, there is not much running, unless there is a problem or a very special situation.*

Coach: What does the quarterback think of doing and actually do almost every time he gets the ball?

Coachee: *Well, he usually is getting rid of it by handing off or passing to someone else!*

Coach: Delegating?

Coachee: *Yes, you could certainly say he is a fast delegator.*

Coach: Could you now talk about what role you may need to play at work, in light of what you have just told me about the difference in those two positions?

Coachee: *Oh, I see. I need to be more of a quarterback, not a running back. I need to be strategic, plan more, to be thinking of who to do the work and how to get the work to them, to delegate and only "run the ball" in more critical or emergency situations.*

Coach: By the way, what happens if a QB runs the ball too much?

Coachee: *Well, at a minimum he gets really tired and compromises his other roles, and he often gets hurt!*

Coach: What may well be the result if you keep running too much?

Coachee: *Well, I am going to be completely exhausted, make mistakes, and probably be taken out, unless I change my mind-set and thinking and act more like a quarterback.*

Coach: What will it take to get you specifically to do this, and what are some time frames you can put in place to make this happen?

The coachee begins to build the action plan at that point with energy, good understanding, and commitment. He also has a very good reminder in the metaphor to keep him on the field and moving toward a touchdown.

I can intensify this same metaphor for the senior, C-suite CEO and ask him questions about moving his mind-set to be the coach of a team or the owner and GM.

Some of the additional questions might be:

Coach: You have told me that you need to be more of a football quarterback, but in your senior role could I suggest even another role?

Coachee: Yes, what?

Coach: What if you were the coach? How many times could you run the ball, even touch the ball or in any way score?

Coachee: Very good point. I would be more limited but still involved, as a more strategic element, to plan, recruit, and to moderate. I could and should work more through my assistant coaches and head coach, who are there on the field and closer to the players.

Coach: But you would still get credit for the WIN.

Coachee: Yes, but for the LOSS too.

Coach: How could you specifically move in that mind-set and what could you commit to, and by when, to make this a reality?

Soccer Player

This metaphor is used with a coachee who not only needs to delegate, but also one who needs to develop others, be more strategic, and move to a higher level of leadership in the organization. For example, one might be a youth soccer coach and possibly a former soccer player. This reframing might help the coachee to motivate others more than "scoring" himself. The result of this learning should be to move the coachee to facilitator and developer of others, rather than being the star or "go-to guy."

> **Coach:** You mentioned earlier that you coached youth soccer and played soccer years ago. Did I get that right?

> **Coachee:** *Yes, I did play soccer as a kid and now I play in an adult soccer league on weekends.*

> **Coach:** There is certainly nothing wrong about taking a soccer ball completely down the field and making a score, is it? But how often is that done in the game of soccer?

> **Coachee:** *Yes, it is fine to do, but it rarely happens.*

Coach: When it is done, who does it?

Coachee: *It is usually done by a younger player with lots of energy, not the older, more experienced player.*

Coach: In terms of your current business challenge that we were discussing, how is this sports picture in any way like business?

Coachee: *Well, yes, in my early career, I was like that younger player, full of energy, taking most of the shots and making most of the goals, but now I am at a different place. I need to be passing, allowing the younger guys to be making the shots and getting the goals. I need to be delegating. I know the game and I know how to do it, but so what? I need to get them to do it now. I need to be more of the strategy guy and set it up, not run the field and wear myself out.*

Coach: Very interesting, and now could I elevate your thinking even further? You are currently a soccer coach now, right? If you took the position of the coach rather than the senior player, could you compare that to your situation at work? What would that look like if you were the coach?

Coachee: *I would be strategizing and communicating, but not making the plays and doing the running around. I would really be delegating and not just talking about my need to do delegating.*

Coach: And how many goals did you score the last game you coached?

Coachee: *None!*

Coach: And is it possible to win, even when you do not personally score any goals?

Coachee: *Yes, and that is the best way!*

Coach: Can I challenge your mind-set by elevating your thinking one more time? Let's say that you were the manager of the team, sitting up in the press box or in the stands. How much would you be able to do to directly affect the score?

Coachee: *Well, the only way I could do it would be to delegate to the max. I would have to communicate, delegate, trust them to do their jobs, and to work through the coach. I would work the system and lead strategically, without micromanaging, taking charge, running onto the field, or controlling the players.*

Coach: Would you specifically articulate that in your real-world business language so I might hear how it would play out if you were really serious about this goal of delegation and leading through others?

At this point, the coachee begins to talk in very practical, measurable, and realistic language, as he states some goals, about which he sounds very passionate. It becomes evident that he gets it, really gets what it might take to play this new role and change his behavior as a leader.

Airliner

This metaphor is often used for a coachee with high potential who is running pretty fast and may be in danger of stalling, derailment, or burnout. This is a classic situation of overplaying a good strength that now needs to be recalibrated or reconsidered.

Coach: You mentioned that you travel a lot. How often are you on airplanes?

Coachee: *Well, I fly almost every week, or at least two to three times a month. It is probably too much, to be honest with you.*

Coach: As we talked about your high potential and the deeply committed behavior that you seem to demonstrate, it reminds me of an airplane. Tell me, what do most airplanes do after they take off and get to about 29,000 feet?

Coachee: *Well, they usually "back off" of the engines, slow down, and level off.*

Coach: Yes, that is the normal approach, but must they level off or could they keep climbing if they wanted? (I usually use my pen, to illustrate the angles of flight as we have this discussion.)

Coachee: I guess they could keep climbing for a while.

Coach: But what would happen if they kept climbing for a long time?

Coachee: I am not sure. I think that they would have some problems, like thin air or something.

Coach: Yes, you are right. The air does get thinner, making it tough to breathe. And the airplane, due to the force of gravity and the science of aeronautics, just stops flying. It is called a stall. The plane stalls; it stops flying upwards and actually starts to fall backwards. It falls backwards until the pilot does a recovery maneuver, by dropping the nose and regaining airspeed. Then the pilot can pull out of the dive and fly again, but much altitude is lost.

Does this metaphor, in any way, remind you of yourself in your current career?

Coachee: Yes, I think that I am like that plane and I am in a stall. I have tried to fly too steeply for too long and I need to level off.

Coach: That does seem to be an option; at least it is for most pilots. And to further this, what do pilots usually do, after they take off and reach their cruising altitude? What do they say to the passengers?

Coachee: Well, they usually level the plane off, slow down, and then they activate the airplane's PA system and talk. They remind the passengers of who they are, who the flight crew is, and then give a brief *weather report, a comment or two about time of arrival, and then they say, "please sit back and enjoy your flight."*

Coach: Interesting. Why do you think they do this?

Coachee: *I am not sure, maybe they are just relaxing the passengers and letting them know that someone intelligent is up there flying the plane and it is time for the crew to get busy doing their work.*

Coach: Maybe they are alleviating the stress that some passengers may feel when flying by calmly communicating the leveling-off maneuver. Could you apply this airplane metaphor further to your situation at work? How is the take-off and flight of an airplane and communication by a pilot in any way a parallel of your professional career?

Coachee: *I am like that plane in several ways. I am still in a very steep climb. I am trying to get higher, faster, and do more than any colleague. I am pretty high right now, but I am also near burnout, or as you said, "the stall." I can feel it. I am high, and feel I want to go further, but the lack of balance in my life suggests that maybe I should slow down and maybe fly a bit more level route for a while. Oh and yes, I should communicate more to the people in my organization, and delegate to them while I do my role. I could even relax more while making progress. Wow, that would be great!*

Coach: What specifically would that look like in your career, schedule, and patterns?

Coachee: *Well, I would now fly more of a regular, level pattern. I would relax some, communicate more, and trust others to do their best. I would delegate more to my crew and not "push the envelope" by flying so fast and at such a steep angle. I would not always be so intensely focused on my success. I would still fly the plane but remember that there are others also on board that need to get to their destinations and enjoy the ride.*

Jet Fighter

When I am coaching someone who is very motivated and driven, I ask them a question about aircraft, which they almost always answer the same way. This is why metaphors work for the coach. When one is clear in one's preferences, then the chances are high that one will answer questions the same way. Thus, the metaphor will usually work. Yet the Socratic style of interaction still empowers coachees to participate, thereby feeling empowered within the metaphor. This empowerment allows them to gain ownership of the picture that is developed, and gives them the feeling that they were actually building much of that picture. This is crucial for them to make an emotional connection with the metaphor so that they will own the words that they offer in response to the coach's tactful leadership.

Coach: If you were going to choose a military aircraft to fly, what would it be? What type of aircraft seems to suit you?

Coachee: *I would choose a fighter, maybe an F-14, F-16, or a Stealth Fighter.*

Coach: I felt sure that you might choose a fighter. A fighter is fast, mission focused, gets to the target quickly and then back home to reload for more missions.

As good as that may be, how many people are usually able to fly in that plane?

Coachee: *One or two.*

Coach: Can this aircraft effectively deal with very precise targets or much larger and broader areas, like a hill or a field?

Coachee: *They are very fast and usually are employed for pretty large targets, unless the target is another airplane moving in the air about as fast as they are.*

Coach: Does your job demand some pretty precise thinking, acting, and usually involving many people?

Coachee: *Yes.*

Coach: What would it look like if you imagined yourself in another type of aircraft, an aircraft with a jet engine and able to move pretty fast but much differently from your initial choice? What if you considered a jet helicopter, specifically like the ones used in the Vietnam conflict? How is a helicopter different from a jet?

Coachee: *It can hold maybe 8-10 people and it can do many things, like evacuate the wounded, bring in men, materials, ammunition, food, etc. It can do surveillance, attack, transport, and support.*

Coach: What else?

Coachee: *Well, it can hover, it is "flexible"; it can do lots of different things.*

Coach: Yes. It can hover or go pretty fast. It is flexible, and has been the key workhorse for many successful missions. It is more vulnerable, but it is very, very useful. Which craft reminds you of your job requirements the most?

Coachee: *Oh, the jet helicopter. It is a lot like my job because it is very multifaceted and sometimes I must be patient and just "hover" until decisions are made or until someone is ready to move forward. I just can't be a jet any longer. That worked well in the early days, but is not working now!*

Coach: There is an emotional component to this metaphor, too. If you ever ask a veteran what he feels when he hears a fast jet fighter coming over, he may tell you that he is a bit worried that the jet pilot might not see him and might possibly, but unintentionally, harm him by what we call "friendly fire." But if you ask a veteran what he feels when he hears a helicopter coming, what do you think he will say?

Coachee: *He will probably say he feels great when he hears that familiar "pop, pop, pop" of a chopper because he feels really supported by the helicopter. Help is coming, supplies are coming, or maybe he is being taken home!*

Coach: What do your employees feel when they hear you coming?

Coachee: *They are probably ducking, fearing and hoping that I do not land near them. They probably feel I am a jet fighter and coming in hard and fast with no time for them, no individual concern or any help coming from me to them.*

Coach: How would you like for them to think or feel when you are coming?

Coachee: *I really need to be more of a helicopter. I want them to feel encouraged, relieved, and supported. I want them to believe I have time for them and that I am not in so much of a hurry that I just "blow by" them.*

I need to stop sometimes and just "hover," ask questions, listen to their answers and solutions, and be able to be very flexible so I can offer what is needed. I need to give assistance and support, or challenge, or maybe just listen to them and take no swift action. I want them to know I care and that I am there for them.

There are many small helicopters on the desks of executives across the country. I was in a CEO's office and he asked me to look on his desk. There on his meticulous desk was a small helicopter. He said, "That little helicopter has been on my desk for 15 years now, and most likely will stay there permanently. I think about the lesson of the helicopter almost daily and try to slow down, to be flexible, and to lead as needed for my team." Somewhere in Canada that small reminder of the helicopter metaphor still sits on that CEO's desk today.

The Three Buckets

Often an executive is overplaying a specific strength. This strength, while very good and useful early in her career, may still be overplayed. Any overplayed strength can often become a weakness or even an irritation, because the one doing the overplaying is usually not aware of her behavior. She is doing what once worked and was needed, and is just repeating past successful behavior. So the task is to coach her into the awareness and into a more strategic behavior pattern.

Coach: Put your career into three buckets: Early—just getting started in your career, Middle—getting into management and significant delegation, and Late—the later stages of your career, beginning to wind down and pass your role on to another. Where are you? What bucket are you in now?

Coachee: *I am in the Middle or between Middle and Late buckets.*

Coach: Tell me about your behavior when you were in the first bucket.

Coachee: *Oh, I was pretty aggressive, on top of everything, very motivated, heads up and in control. I was very active and pretty competitive and independent.*

Coach: Thinking about your day-to-day behavior, what bucket do you seem to be operating in?

Coachee: *Well, my behavior is still Early–career behavior.*

Coach: Yes, but what bucket did you tell me you were in?

Coachee: *Hmmm, I said Middle to Late.*

Coach: What would your behavior look like if you were really living in the Middle–career bucket?

Coachee: *Well, I would be more strategic, less tactical, calmer, and not chasing every issue or battle. I would be doing more delegating and less putting out of the fires...*

Coach: What would it take to get you to that type of behavior? Could we set some goals for your progress and to correct your focus in these strategic days?

Golf Grip

Often an executive is a golfer, at some level, and can identify with this metaphor when his behavior pattern is being overly focused, up tight, and too controlling.

Coach: What sport do you like to play? (This can work with golf, baseball, hockey, even painting.)

Coachee: *I prefer golf, but I am not very good.*

Coach: Well, I am not a big golfer, but lots of my coachees are and they talk about the game a lot. Since you are the golfer here, tell me: What does squeezing or holding the club really tight do for your shot?

Coachee: *Well, not much. It actually hurts it, and the shot has less distance and less accuracy.*

Coach: Do you mean if a golfer was really conscientious, very serious about his game, and was trying hard to do his best and was squeezing his club as a result of his intense effort, it might be less effective rather than more effective?

Coachee: *Oh yes, definitely.*

Coach: How should you hold the club?

Coachee: *You should hold it loosely, just enough to get a natural swing and yet not let go of the club.*

Coach: How might your holding on tight, controlling, or just being tense at your job compare to this holding of a club?

Coachee: *Oh, I can see how I am just like that at work. I am pretty controlling, tense, and sometimes trying too hard.*

Coach: What is the result of that behavior in your work?

Coachee: *I have not considered that before. It is just how I have always operated, not letting anything get by me, trying really hard to do my best.*

Coach: So what has the result been?

Coachee: *Lately, it has not been so good, but I couldn't work any harder.*

Coach: That may have been perfect behavior in the early days or at some challenging times in your professional career, but if you were to enjoy your career more and get more from your efforts, what would that look like?

Coachee: *Well, just like that grip, I need to relax, not be so tense, and just act more easy and natural.*

Coach: What might be the result of that approach at work?

Coachee: *For one, people might stop exiting my department. I could ease up some and even enjoy work and not worry and compete so much. And who knows, I might just do better. At least I would enjoy the "game" more.*

Coach: Let's make some specific goals on how to do just that.

The Overplayed Strength

This metaphor is often used with "The Three Buckets," but it is actually better when the coachee develops the metaphor and then makes the connection to himself.

> **Coach:** What is wrong with the strengths that you display in your job? You are fast, insightful, and dynamic with a bias for action, and you usually get results, right?
>
> **Coachee:** *Yes, usually I am the "go-to guy" on the sales side and have been for years.*
>
> **Coach:** Is that as good as it is, working for you?
>
> **Coachee:** *I think so, but not sure. Something seems a bit out of balance and I am often told to be more strategic.*
>
> **Coach:** Tell me more. What might that look like to you?

Coachee: *I guess I would delegate more, and not always be the productive, go-to guy.*

Coach: Could I get you to tell me about an athlete who has a particular strength, like maybe a quarterback who is good at passing the ball or a pitcher who has a great fastball? Is there anything fundamentally wrong with such a strength, skill, or talent?

Coachee: *No, there's nothing wrong with being good at what you do.*

Coach: But what if he overuses such a great strength? He gets known for it and so, for identity's sake, just defaults to his strength and uses it all of the time.

Coachee: *He would probably burn out, or maybe get injured. He would possibly get tired with no variety and then others would anticipate his moves, and then use his strength against him, and that would decrease his impact and value to the team.*

Coach: Would you parallel that picture to your role at work currently?

Coachee: *That is me exactly. I am so action oriented that it has become my identity, my life, and my default behavior.*

Coach: What do you think would be the result of continuing at this pace?

Coachee: *I will probably burn out soon, or maybe get discouraged or angry; I could get tired with no variety and then others would anticipate my moves. I would become too predictable, almost mechanical, and then others might use this against me. My impact and value to the team and my employees would decrease.*

Coach: Can you articulate specifically what you can do to avoid this pattern or behavior to better modulate that overplayed strength?

The Wolves

During a coaching conversation it became obvious that my coachee is successful, a former high potential that is now at full speed and yet beginning to find too much on her plate in the office. I can sense the probability that she is not delegating sufficiently and beginning to move toward ineffectiveness. This valuable coachee is suffering from never quite seeing her protective mentality. Though well intended, the impact or consequence is to prevent direct reports' development, growth, and maturity. In order to confirm my suspicion and to allow her to also see her situation in the mirror of the question, I ask:

Coach: One of my favorite questions when I meet an efficient executive like you, with such a strong track record, is this: In the early days, when you were first in the management ranks, did they ever "throw you in there with the wolves"? You know, entrust you with some pretty big challenges, some assignments with some element of risk?

Coachee: *Yes!*

(By the way, a coach can also get an estimate of how large those early challenges were from the emphasis and the speed with which the coachee chooses to answer that question. Some will very quickly and emphatically say, "Yes!" Some will pause and be more thoughtful…but 9 out of 10 do answer affirmatively.)

Coach: That is a very common response. Almost all successful coachees with similar positions answer "yes" to that question, and I anticipated that you would too. But here is the bigger question: Presently, do you frequently put your direct reports in there with the wolves?

(Wait for the answer.)

Coachee: *I just realized that I don't do that!*

Coach: Now, let me get this straight. You were, in your early days, trusted with some very large challenges with some risk. But you are telling me that the very environment that you were afforded and trusted with and the situations that allowed you to grow and to become the leader you are today are being withheld, by you, from your direct reports?

Coachee: *I have never thought of it that way, until now! I am.*

(This is a pretty large discovery for most executives, and it is critical that they make the discovery through your questions.)

Coach: It is very common for a good leader to do what you are currently doing; but still a problem. If you continue to do what you have described, what will be the result on your direct reports?

Coachee: *They will not grow and develop. They will not be able to take the larger roles ahead of them. Come to think of it, I have been doing the large assignments and keeping them from significant portions of the work.*

Coach: What will be the result of your continued behavior on you?

Coachee: *I will probably crash or just burn out!*

(Again, this is a very critical discovery for the executive and it is very important to hear her verbalize the potential result of her continued behaviors.)

Coach: I want you to know that this admission is significant, and I have heard you say that you have realized that your behavior is ineffective in the long run. You recognize that to continue this pattern will not allow for development and may even cripple your direct reports, organizationally. And for you, the result may be career derailment or failure in some way. Is this what you are saying?

I want you to know this is so common for a number of reasons. You probably well remember the "wolves," with the teeth and the pain. Since you are a leader, with a heart, you probably do not want your direct reports to feel that pain the way you did. Am I right?

Coachee: *Yes, I guess so.*

Coach: It is either that or the fact that it is a bit irrational to ease up and change styles to a more delegating style, when being a sole performer and a high producer has always worked so well in the past for you. It may also be based on some pride that you have not identified. You may feel that you took the "wolves" and survived, but they just could not handle them. Which is it?

Coachee: *No, really, I just have not realized that I am actually doing this. Maybe I am not sure of my motives, but I see clearly now that I need to just trust them, put them in there with the "wolves," delegate a lot more to them, and not do so much of the work!*

Coach: Again, let me remind you that the athletic world and the military world, along with many professional training situations, do care for the trainees. They choose to put them in situations that may make the trainee feel like they are going to fail, go under, or possibly die, but the intent is to not actually allow them to fail. Do you remember those days? Perhaps some wise manager was there, delegating to you, but willing to catch you, support you or rescue you, but nonetheless, you were in a challenging place, feeling lots of pressure, and you performed!

Is it time you created the same environment for your direct reports?

Coachee: *Yes! It is not only time, it is way past time. I have been shielding them, hovering over them, and just not allowing them to sink, swim, or shine.*

Coach: Great! So now what are some of your specific goals as you think of this new, more significant delegation mind-set? What will you do differently as you get back to the office? When will you start? What will be the results that you can measure?

Again, the key to metaphors that work is using some comparison that the coachees are familiar with, and then asking them some basic question about that idea or sport. Then they can tell you about the concept or sport. A significant amount of the discussion can be applied to the coaching session. Metaphors can underline and illustrate the key points of the discussion, especially if the coach is wise enough to use *The Master Coach Model* and to ask the coachee to make the connections, comparisons, and applications.

COACHING INSIGHTS

- Executives with three or more children seem to have a better capacity to manage. Also, illustrations and metaphors with children are very effective.

- Leaders with a faith perspective seem to inherently understand more servant-oriented leadership and the essence of what is known about leadership skills and practices.

- Leaders tend to manage with a style of leadership that often resembles their major sport/position.

- Leaders' management style often reflects the age of their children. Those with younger children are often doing too much structuring and "hand holding." Those with teens are somewhat less involved and at times disconnected. Those who have launched their children often have a better understanding of the need to move others to self-sufficiency and to independence.

- Leadership in the home can be an application to business or an extension of leadership learning. The practice of management in the home or church can be very transferable to the corporate world.

- Support is necessary at all levels of leadership. Those who are gifted to lead often are in need of someone to support them and supply administration and other follow-up behaviors.

- The active mind produces behavioral change. The more active the learner's mind, the more effective the learning tends to be and the greater the behavioral change. The most effective way to stimulate the learner's mind is with questions.

- The third time a question is asked, the more likely the truth is offered. Just try asking someone how they are doing. Most of the time you get, "Fine!" If you ask the same question in a slightly different way, or just repeat the same one, you will often get a different and more truthful response.

- Never hesitate to ask the same question two or three times. The first question that a coachee hears is often discounted or disregarded as simply basic social politeness.

- Questions about behavior and significance can often be dismissed as just curiosity or, worse, as insincerity. They are some of the best questions to get the coachee to think and reason at a deeper level.

- Rarely coach an instance, unless the instance concerns moral, legal, or ethical violations. But always coach a pattern. Simply noticing the pattern of absenteeism, tardiness, or other observable behavior can be helpful feedback to the coachee and also a great place to enter a coaching interaction.

- When a coachee asks for the coach to give his insights, ideas, feedback, or summary, it often is a hook to get the coach to do the work. If you defer your thoughts until the coachee has put his on the table, he will rarely return to press for the insight of the coach.

● The coach should not work harder than the coachee! Actually this is a bit of a misnomer in that coaching can be hard work. The mind-set is critical and the questions are some of the hardest work. But in terms of the solution and the action plan, this is primarily directed at whose work, whose career, and who has to do the execution?

● "Silence is Golden"! Especially when the coachee is thinking, solving, and considering a plan of action. Allow for this "golden silence" or the coach will end up working more trying to sell ideas, then owning the solution and action plans.

● Coaching, as in sales, follows with a pause. The next one to speak usually loses. This can be true in coaching unless the next one to speak asks a great question.

● When the coach offers ideas, they should be few, and even then mostly in the form of a question. The ideas offered by the coach are unfortunately owned by the coach and must be sold to the coachee. Ideas by the coachee are fortunately owned by the coachee and are much more empowering and have a greater chance for success.

● When the coach's ideas are offered, they also become the source of blame if and when the ideas do not succeed.

● In the event that the coachee gets stuck, having no ideas or solutions, the coach has a decision: wait until the coachee has had time to consider, research, etc., or provide a solution. The long-term result may be a lesson in how to fish, rather than just handing out another fish.

TOOLS IN COACHING

Interpersonal skills and particularly the ability to communicate interest and concern for others is a critical ability for a coach. One of the most valuable ways I have found to make initial connections and also to show interest is the FORM method. This tool is also useful to assist the more task-oriented and mission-oriented managers, as they are not often inclined to make interpersonal connections or to do anything other than move toward task and accomplish the mission.

THE FORM MODEL

This approach utilizes the Master Coach emphasis on asking questions and focuses on the coachee.

F – FAMILY

The initial questions are around family: questions like, "How's the family?" This is a more general question that focuses on the big picture. General questions are very open-ended such as, "How's life?" or "How are things going?" Any general question is a good place to start. The question of family may seem too personal for some, but most of us have a family, or can comfortably respond to sincere questions about people to whom we are related.

The secondary reason for the questions is for the coach to learn to observe and respond to the way the coachee answers the questions. This will be discussed later in this model.

O – ORGANIZATION

The second step in this method of questioning is to ask about organization: for example: "How is work?" "How is the business, the department, the task you are working on, the current challenge ...?" These questions about the organization are usually pretty comfortable and the coachee can easily respond.

R – RECREATION

The third step is questions around recreation: "So what have you done for fun lately?" "Have you taken your vacation?" "When is your vacation?" "When is your next trip?" These questions are centered upon activities they have done in nonworking time or family recreation.

M – MISSION OR MEANING

The final stage of questions is mission or meaning. These are questions about the issues that need to be discussed.

The point is that the coach who uses the above method to initiate communications may find:

(1) a better overall relationship with the coachee,

(2) a deeper insight into the thoughts and feelings of the coachee, and

(3) an opportunity to uncover some of the real issues or latent issues.

When I ask coachees to be honest about how often, during communication with their team or peers, they begin with the mission, most say they do so most of the time, if not always. They do so because of their efficient mind-set trained to get to the point and get things done. When they are encouraged to use the FORM method of initiating communication, or at least to use one or two of the key questions before getting to the mission, the usual response is "I can do that, and it is certainly worth the try." They also report that the result is very significant. The employees or peers tell the coachees that they feel they are showing more care and concern, and are listening better. The process often works as follows (note the twist in the honesty by the time the interaction gets to the letter R–Recreation). The coachee usually demonstrates more honesty and openness by the third question.

Coach: So how are you, and how's the family?

Coachee: Fine.

Coach: How is the job?

Coachee: Oh, pretty good. We are still making progress with the new assignment and keeping on track with the daily assignments.

Coach: Have you had any fun lately? Have you taken any vacations or enjoyable trips?

Coachee: Well, since you asked, we have been traveling a great deal with the family. My son is a serious hockey player.

Coach: Oh, that's interesting. Has he been winning games and enjoying the season?

Coachee: *Yes, he has been winning, and just last night he won a big game, but he broke his arm. We were in the E.R. till 2 a.m.*

Now, what is interesting is that when asked about family, what did the coachee say? Often the coachee will not answer completely to the initial questions, most likely because the coach may not be perceived as sincere or interested in the full answer. By the time the coach asks five or more questions, the coachee is much more likely to fully or truthfully respond to the question and the coach now gets a much more complete picture.

The importance of this method and what the conversation teaches is that the true emotional state of the coachee is very important to know. Is it critical to know the initial mind-set or openness of the coachee, if productive coaching is to result? A more open and willing mind, of course, makes more progress than a resistant or distracted mind.

Earlier I mentioned the importance of the coach observing the coachee, reading the coachee's behavior, and responding appropriately. If the coach discerns that the coachee is not open, or fully open to the coaching, it is usually wise to refocus or postpone the coaching. Refocus by dealing with the presenting issue, distraction, or problem; or postpone until the coachee is in a better place to make progress through the interactive and interrogative coaching process. When this is not possible, the coach may request that the coachee isolate or mentally put aside the current challenge or frustration and allow them both to focus on the coaching issue or bigger issue that must be attended to. Sometimes the coachee can and is more than willing to do so. Oftentimes he simply needs a moment to re-focus, and then he is ready to go forward with coaching. To simply ignore the distraction or other challenge may not be productive, and to press forward simply because you are the coach and had this time scheduled is also unwise.

REPHRASING

Listening is critical to coaching. One skill to demonstrate excellent listening is to use the coaching tool of rephrasing. This is simply briefly restating the essence and key bullet points of what the coachee just said to demonstrate that you are indeed listening. This is not only convincing, it is powerful. It is convincing because only those who truly listen can restate what has been communicated. It is powerful for several reasons. When one has just been accurately heard and restated, the result is trust. The trust increases and the comfort of the coaching relationship increases. This is the key to leveraging what happens next.

Often when I restate, I ask a question like, "Is that right, or a good summary of what you told me?" Now, one might think that senior executives, for the sake of efficiency, would retort, "Of course, that is what I just told you!" but that has never occurred in any of my coaching sessions. On the contrary, the more useful and powerful response is very surprising. When I am disciplined enough to simply restate, to check for understanding, and then be silent, it happens. After I ask, "Did I get it right?" the coachee often says, "Yes, exactly," or "Absolutely." These are golden responses and it is the goal to pull them whenever possible, for it is the precursor to their next statement. As I wait, they often say, "And you know what, the real issue is ...!" That is a win. Whenever they say the real issue, or the big struggle, or the bottom line concern is ..., then we are leveraging the questions, the moment, and, yes, even the time. For what seemed at first blush to be ineffective has jumped to a keynote and thus become most effective and efficient as well.

Sometimes after my attempt to restate or rephrase I ask the question, "Did I get it right?" and they surprise me with, "No, not exactly," then they explain and make it clearer. Either response brings us closer to the full story and a clearer picture in my mind and theirs. As they walk on into the issue, this time they go with a coach, someone to listen and help them sort out right or real issues. They do not go alone, and they are more willing to share the whole story, to take time to break it down, to observe the patterns, and to find that really useful approach to the right perspective or solution.

IN THE MOMENT

Another tool that has been most helpful in my coaching sessions is what I refer to as "in-the-moment" coaching. This is catching the very moment when the coachee is in some way demonstrating or acting out the very behavior with which you are concerned.

An example:

Coachee: *I know we have talked about my tendency to quickly judge and to disagree with something, but I am not so sure about that. I think that I am very open-minded and someone who tries to listen, consider, and think through an option or idea.*

Coach: That seemed to be a fast judgment in the way you disagreed with me. Do you do that often?

(Here the coach has "turned on the light" or held up the mirror to show the coachee that they just did it, "in the moment.")

Less obvious, but still "in the moment":

Coachee: *I am concerned about my relationship and influencing skills. Those around me seem to not see me as warm and caring as I see my-self. They give feedback to me that I am somehow cool and distant in some of my interactions.*

Coach: Can I give you some "in-the-moment" feedback? Do you often interact with them the same way you interact with me, like we are doing today?

Coachee: *Well, yes, I guess so. Why do you ask?*

Coach: Do you often use about the same amount of introductory talk when you first meet with them and about the same amount of eye contact?

Coachee: *Yes, but again, where are you going with this?*

Coach: (Silence)

Coachee: *So, you are thinking that my short greeting, my to-the-point behavior and limited eye contact is carrying more of the message than the content of my words?*

Coach: That is very possible. If so, what would you like your behavior to be?

Coachee: *I would prefer to take more time to connect, to talk a few minutes about general topics, maybe ask a few questions to see what emerges and maybe even the topic I wanted to address will come up. About the eye contact, I am not sure.*

Coach: May I offer that you seem to look somewhere just off to my right, your left, to formulate your words? Then you seem to glance my way about mid-sentence and then your eye contact drops off again. Are you aware of that?

Coachee: *Why, no, not at all!*

Coach: What would you prefer your behavior to be like in this exchange and with those you want to connect with and those you want to influence? And specifically, what will your steps of action be?

Coachee: *I would prefer to make a better connection and to have more influence by more eye contact, by more "small talk" at first. Then I would like to continue more increasing eye contact to make sure they know I am interested, focused, and not detached. I will begin this with my family and staff, and then seek feedback about my progress each week on Fridays.*

Coach: Our words often describe the value we place on something. "Small" often belies one's view of the early part of a conversation as less important and possibly insignificant, even dispensable. Does that at all describe how you have been thinking about such introductory interactions with those you work with?

Coachee: *You sure have me there…I like to simply get to the point, you know, the really important content, the business data that we came to discuss.*

Coach: I understand, but didn't you tell me that your concern and your goal is to communicate and to have more influence, not just to do business?

Coachee: *Yes, that is right.*

Coach: Then I would love to offer you a new term, a new way of thinking about introductory comments, or as you have called it, "small talk." I call it "bridge talk"! Why do you think I would call it that?

Coachee: Oh, I guess that "bridge" is a way to think of making a connection, of getting from the early talk to the more important and more actionable part of the discussion. But in thinking of the bridge, like any bridge, it is pretty important, especially if they have "built a moat" or have some resistance to having the meeting or discussion.

Coach: Very good. If you can see in the early moments of the "bridge talk" that they are hesitant or resistant in some way, what can you do that might be effective?

Coachee: I could use the "in-the-moment" technique. If I see them looking disinterested or unmotivated, I could ask them if they are aware of their behavior, and to explore with them what might be causing that behavior, for it might be me!

Coach: Good insight. I'd love to hear about your progress.

WHEN LOST, ASK THE COACHEE

Another tool is the question about the question! Often in a coaching interaction, the coach may be lost. The coach can also use this tool to reflect or summarize what has happened so far. This tool is to simply ask the coachee. This can help the coach catch up and provide transformational summary or insight.

Coach: What question would be good for me to ask you, that I have not yet asked you?

Coachee: *(pause) You probably need to ask me about why I have not made any progress in this area before now. I have been aware of this, but just have not made it my priority.*

Coach: Any ideas on what has kept this so low on the priority list? What has prevented you from progress? If we surface that, maybe we can be of help in getting you moving toward success.

Coachee: *The other priorities just seem to crowd this out. The urgent things push out what is important.*

Coach: If you were able to make a list and see how far down that priority is, would that help?

Coachee: *Yes.*

Coach: What else might help you for your success?

THE TIME OUT

Often the coachee, when asked a good question, is stuck or has not had time to frame a response. The coachee says, "I don't know." This is dangerously close to them "reversing the tables" and asking the coach for an answer or solution and "hooking" the coach to do the work.

Coach: So what are your thoughts toward a solution with this challenge?

Coachee: *I don't know, what do you think, boss?*

Coach: It sounds like you need some time to think or research this concept. I may have some thoughts, but whose role is this?

Coachee: *Well, mine, but you've done this before.*

Coach: Yes, but my knowledge and experience is a bit dated. My solutions may be less valid, and besides, I'd love to hear your best thinking and ideas! Why don't you think about this until tomorrow morning and we can talk again. By the way, would you also, along with the solutions, think about how it would be beneficial if you are able to come up with an excellent solution?

Coachee: *Wow, sounds like I have some homework. Can we meet tomorrow at noon?*

Coach: I am looking forward to it!

Conclusion

In summary, *The Master Coach Model* is a question-centered approach, focused on the coachee, to move toward a solution that the coachee has owned and authored. The process of connection, clarification, and commitment results in an empowered coachee with a specific plan of action. When possible, a memorable metaphor can make the solution come alive and remain in the category marked: Unforgettable.

48137584R00049

Made in the USA
Charleston, SC
25 October 2015